A Comparative Study of E.M. Forster's *MAURICE*

A Comparative Study of E.M. Forster's *MAURICE*

Ruby Roy

GenNext Publication

ISBN : 978-93-8022-256-1

Price : ₹ 250

First Published, 2015

Published by :

Gennext Publications
23, Main Ansari Road,
Dariyaganj, New Delhi-110002
Ph. : 23282060, 23261060
E-mail: gennext@hotmail.com

Laser Typesetting : Shubham Printers, Delhi

Printed at : G. Print Process, Delhi

Cataloging in Publication Data—DK
Courtesy: D.K. Agencies (P) Ltd. <docinfo@dkagencies.com>

Roy, Ruby, author.
A comparative study of E.M. Forster's Maurice / Ruby Roy.
pages cm
Includes bibliographical references (pages).
ISBN 9789380222561

1. Forster, E. M. (Edward Morgan), 1879-1970. Maurice. I. Title. II. Title: Maurice.

DDC 823.912 23

Contents

Acknowledgements

This book is a modest attempt on my part to highlight critical aspects of E.M. Forster's novel *Maurice* in relation with his other novels.

I would like to express my gratitude to the Principal Sir Dr Satendra Kumar Joshi of Satyawati College (Evening) for his constant encouragement and support.

My heart felt thanks to my Ph.d. supervisor Dr Manjari Agarwal and my mentor Dr R.K. Agarwal, Professor and Ex-Head, Department of English (Dr B.R. Ambedkar University, Agra) for their valuable guidance.

Last but not the least, I must mention that my father Shalil Roy, my mother Anima Roy and my brother Shomor Roy, who have encouraged me to write this book and have stood as the greatest source of inspiration in my honest and sincene endeavour the exercise.

RUBY ROY

Introduction

E.M. Forster developed and conceived the idea of his novel *Maurice* between 1913 and 1914. However it was not published during Forster's lifetime when it appeared in 1917, a good deal of literary controversy ensued. The problematic aspect about this novel originated with E.M. Forster being confused about this particular piece of work. According to an Introduction by P.N. Furbank, the novel was revised in 1919, and 1932, in "once more, fairly drastically, in 1959-1960" Forster created another mystery by scrawling "publishable-but worth it" on the cover of the neatly prepared 1960 manuscript, and most reviewers have since tried to sort out this question by author.

The publication of this novel invited a lot of literary and non-literary criticism. First of all, one must not forget the fact of the novel's suppression during the author's lifetime. The novel is primarily concerned with illustrating Forster's point of view about homosexuality being normal leading to happily ever after conclusion of gay relationshp. In 1914, this idea was unacceptable, except perhaps in very sophisticated circles. Philip Toynbee encapsulates the situation succinctly when he commented about the novel:

> The Wilde case was still reverberating
> and English homosexuals were living in
> greater fear, shame and distress than
> they had done even in the middle of
> the nineteenth century.

The lightest sentence for the alternate sexual orientation was still ten years in prison. According to Forster's biographers, he was very close to his Victorian ancestors, and his middle-class relatives. If one considers his regard for tradition and his attachment to his famly, censure of his refusal to print becomes impossible. The benefit he may have done to the world in speeding change of laws and attitudes would have been negligible in his eyes, if it involved dire consequences for the Forster and Thornton.

By 1967, his mother and other relatives were dead; furthermore, the Wolfenden report revising sexual laws had been accepted, and he could, if he wished, have published the novel. According to Furbank

> **Friends actually suggested it, but he firmly refused...Also, the book had become rather remote to him. He said he was less interested now in the theme of salvation, the rescuer from 'otherwhere'; he thought it was a 'fake.'**

This explanation does not seem satisfactory; if he felt so remote he could have destroyed the manuscript, instead of putting so much effort in preparing it so carefully for publication. As a reader, one can speculate that the "eyes of the world", the conventionality that Forster denounces in each of his works, also affected his own view of the world. The bourgeois values associated with "Sawston" in *Where Angels Fear to Tread* and *The Longest Journey* are just as much a part of Forster's world-picture as the "Cambridge" ideals of "eccentricity" and freedom that these novels present. One can surmise that Forster could never resolve feelings about his strong little radical novel. The rest of his fiction also complement or comment on this posthumous publication. Keeping in mind, Forster's love for secrets and surprises, an interesting theory can be developed.

One senses, a sort of rebirth for Forster through the posthumous publication of a flawed, semi-autobiographical novel. The theme of immortality is present in his major works of fiction. *In the Longest Journey*, Rickie and his deformed daughter both die, but their name and memory live on in the form of Stephen Wonham's child. In *A Passage to India*, Moore live on through her children, and in the memory of those she befriended in India. In *Where Angels Fear to Tread*, much of the plot involves Gino's desire for a son, and the future of that child. In *Howards End*, the house preserve both the life of England, and the memory of Wilcox. In any case, if Forster considered his own life as a story, *Maurice* provides it with an excellent conclusion.

Chapter 1

Art and Artist

Maurice as a novel invites many complex interpretations. The shadow of the novelist intrudes upon our analysis at every turn. E.M. Forster, being of public person complicates matters more as the text itself contains brief autobiographical note, which we cannot easily dismiss. The current trend of studying Forster's personal philosophy misleads any thorough examination of his texts. It becomes convenient to forget the original novel, and see only the author who wrote it. Any author's biography can work as an indicator towards hidden facets of a novel but at the same time it can also distort the text. It is dangerous to draw too many parellels between the writer's experiences and those of characters, the novel would be reduced to what Forster himself once described as a "pathological tract." It is a sorry fact that most embarrssing details of Forster's life came to surface after his death. Alfred Borrello comments:

> **Almost from the moment of his death,**
> **Friends whom he cheirshed in life,**
> **raced into print to reveal the dark**
> **corners of his private life which he**
> **had successfully concealed from the**
> **general public.**

If Borrello considers Forster's personal life should not be so publicly revealed then he could be wrong here but guarding against sensationalism or irrelevant facets of author's life then his remarks are justified.

Thus, attempting to situate *Maurice* in a suitable slot in Forster's canon can lead to misinterpretations. Out of IX novels of Forster, it is easy to forget about *Maurice,* as it is not a masterpiece according to critics in comparison with other works of Forster. As 21st century readers, we can consider the novel as an autonomous artistic structure as well as a new link in the chain of existing works by Forster.

Seeing Forster's work as a whole has often meant tracing a chronological development in his writings. One can view his early works as steps in the production of his later works. Wilfred Stone's seminal work *The Cave and the Mountain* traces out the evolution of Forster as a writer. He considers the novels as "dramatic instalments in the story of Forster's own struggle for selfhood-and a myth to support it." Stone concludes his study saying "between the stories and *A Passage to India,* there is an evolution of the artist from a child to a man's estate." It is a noteworthy fact that Forster published four novels in rapid succession, starting with *Where Angels Fear to Tread* in 1905. He then paused for fourteen years between *Howards* (1910) and *A Passage to India* (1924). At the age of 45 with half of his life still to come, he stopped totally publishing novels. This does not mean that subsequent creative works of Forster did not appear at all According to Miss Kirkpatrick's bibliography, he went on to publish over four hundred pieces, including two biographies, two pageants, a libretto, and many critical articles. One of Forster's friend said, "When Forster stopped writing novels, he became a sage." Intelligent readers did not believe the apparent reasons of his silence which according to Forster was his drying up creativity. By the sixties, two critical view points had emerged, one group explained his silence as a disillusionment with contemporary modern society, while the second considered psychological repression as a cause of his abandonment of fiction.

Forster in his 1959 television interview confirmed the first view:

> I think one of the reasons why I stopped writing novels is that the social aspect of the world changed so much. I had been accustomed to write about the old-fashioned world with its homes and its family life and its comparative peace, All that went, and though I can think about the new world, I cannot put it into fiction.

Critics who believe this explanation feel the Forster's novels are about a pre-war, Edwardian universe, *Richard Martin, The Love that Failed, (*The Hague-Paris : Mouton and Co., 1974*)* Those who agree with the second reason for Forster's detachment from fiction writing feel the issue of homosexuality is ambiguously present in the five published works.

To throw light on this aspect, one has to seek out any new information about Forster after his death. This is not an easy task. The first public statement of his homosexuality did not occur until two months after his death, on a radio programme on the BBC (August, 1970). But this was not a shocking fact for many of his friends and critics, who were already aware of the orientation of Forster "Forster was himself a homosexual and for many years a fully practicing one". It was already known to Forster's close friends that he had written a novel which dealt with homosexual relationship and had to be published only after his death. Furthermore, the theme of homosexuality in the previous fiction of Forster had been explored; thus the posthumous works merely encouraged a critical stance which already existed. Stone, for example, talked about Rickie's "Latent homosexuality", in 1966. Since the publication of *Maurice*, , there is a however tendency for critics to simply imagine homosexual relationship among Forster's fictional characters. This critical trend of finding homosexual characters in Forster's fiction, made Borrello remark:

> One shudders to think what will be
> made of the Fielding-Aziz friendship
> in *A Passage to India*.

Clearly, there is a requirement for a thorough exploration of the writer's fiction.

Today, we have the information that Forster wrote *Maurice* during the fourteen year gap between *Howard's* End *and A Passage to India*. Adding to that, his private papers bring also to light about his hidden frustration with the topic of heterosexual love; this nugget of information provides one more substantial explanation of his abadonment of publishable fiction. Forster hated the conditions of his times and longed for the freedom of expression, which would enable him talk about anything and everything under the sun. He fought against censorship by attending tribunals, and making speeches. He defended the publication of D.H. *Lawence's Lady Chatterley's Lover,* Radcliffe Hall's lesbian novel, *The Well of Loneliness*, and other controversial novels. According to Forster, a writer needs an audience, and the freedom to say what he wants, or he becomes "afraid to feel." Clearly, this scare affected his own writing sensibility. He says in his private notes, "Having sat for an hour in vain trying to write a play will analyse cause of my own sterility.... I shall never write another novel after it (*A Passage*)-My patience with ordinary people has given out" (Letter, Aug 1, 1923). There is definitely a hint of tragic writer's self which could not deal with restrictive atmosphere, and one wonders what he may have written in a free society.

There is certainly a link between Forster's feelings about homosexuality and his major theme, which Lionel Trilling accurately defines as a research into the "profound pathology" of "the heart untrained and untutored–The heart checked too early in its natural possible growth." According to Trilling, Forster's miserable experiences at school led to his interest in the growth of the heart. In the novel, *Maurice* feels tormented as a homosexual because of the traditional Education which is ambiguous enough. In "Notes on the English character" (1920), Forster shows a hatred for the British public-school system for sending boys out into the world "Well-developed bodies, fairly developed minds and undeveloped hearts" Rose Macaulay comments about the essay, "This public school business is rather perplexing. Can it really be that boys sent to live together for a few years to do lessons and play games, turn into something quite different from what they would have turned into if they had lived at home and attended day schools?" Forster would have agreed with Macaulay.

In an article named "*Society and the Homosexual*: The Abominable Crime (1953), Forster says "Certainly, the segregation of the sexes in boarding schools seems designated to increase homosexuality..." Clearly, then, Forster's dislike for British public-school system can be more understood in the context of his concern for the homosexual's plight in society. Similarly, his views about other issues can be explained in terms of various aspects of his complex view of homosexuality. His scepticism about marriage, clergyman (organised religion), education, school-trachers, and other authorities can be teaced back to his personal hatred of contemporary society. Malcolm Bradbury lightly observes:

> **The publication of Maurice is bound to remind us vigorously of the basis in**

> his personal life and passion from which writing arose; it gives a local justification for his liberalism and his attitude toward human feeling, toward emancipating personal relationships, the growth of the heart.

So when we understand which personal hurt motivated Forster, his texts give out new meanings. George Steiner writes :

> A number of his most famous dicta It is better to betray one's country than a friend, 'only connect'-take on a more restricted, shriller ambience.

Although Steiner may be right in his interpretation still no matter what the author's personal life was, we must finally judge the literary product, as an independent thing in the purified world of art. A literary critic must focus on the text itself. Forster himself knew this, and often warned reader about it. In the beginning, he pleaded for objective literary criticism. He questions "Do You like to know who a book's by?", In "Anonymitiy : An Inquiry", and "Art for Art's sake", he is against much emphasis on writer's personality/life while analysing his works. These essays seem prophetic now when we talk about his work. Even the critics got bored with biographical criticism, for example Elizabath Bowen says :

> The author of *Where Angels fear to Tread* had already as much authority as the author of *A Passage to India.*

One can detect a sense of boredom with the issue of Forster's growth in his novels: She would much rather read the books.

Forster in one of his television interviews talked about this need to separate author's life from his fiction. He says, "I am more interested in achievement than in advance or decline from it; and I am more interested in works than in authors. The paternal wish of critics to show how a writer dropped off or picked up as he went along seems to be misplaced."

Since the publication of the posthumous work, it has become increasingly difficult to ignore the issue of Forster's development. Furthermore, it is necessary to investigate the relevance of information not found within the texts themselves, in order to achieve a balanced view of his art. Thus, it becomes necessary for critics to strike a balance between these two approaches when analysing a semi–autobiographical novel like *Maurice*.

Chapter 2

Repression of the Hero

Maurice can be considered a queer thesis novel as the idea of homosexuality stands at the center of the book. Other themes and chacacterisation do not have any place in it and didactic purpose rigorously control each incident. Furbank writes :

> **Forster needed to affirm, without possibility of retreat, that love of this kind could be ennobling.**

Forster discusses his writing in *Aspects of the Novel*, when he talks about stories in which "Characters have to fall in with something else in the novel...and have, of course, to modify their make-up accordingly." One can sense Forster creating a "pattern" in mind to which he sacrifices other elements in fiction, and produces "a book of the rigid type a book with a unity, and in this sense an easy book". *Maruice,* with all the aspects pointing out to a single idea is precisely this type of book, and at many points, the sacrifices made are too great. Forster's other novels have character development in a free environment and broader themes too. In *Maurice,* we see a author-narrator with an idee fixe. He moulds each part of the book to show the need for a new outlook towards homosexuality.

In order to encourage this outlook, Forster in the novel gives us a representative Bitish figure, who also happens to be homosexual. All of the English masculine characters in Forster's novels share some of the national traits that are discussed "Notes on the English character" but only Maurice possesses them all. He is even physically strong, which is a unique quality among Forsterian heroes. But when one compares him to Philip, Rickie, Henry Wilcox or Fielding, he appears wooden. Because of his aim to deliver a social message, Forster provides us with a hero, who is occasionally more stereotype than archeype, more "flat" than "round". He is a product of the middle class, and of the public school system: On prize day we are told that he is honoured because he is 'average'. A surprising fact what has happened to Forster's usual subflety. One can see thike the Englishman of 'Notes' Who has been taught in pubic school system that feeling is bad form", Maurice gets a repressive education and emerges in a "bewildered" state. Basically, he is confused. It seems that the picture of English muddledom could not be more complete. Maurice is a mere receptacle for the typically "English emotions" which Forster compared to Fish "moving far below" distorted and obscure."

Reading the text, a perceptive reader can find certain vivid details which stand out in the sea of description of Maurice Hall. For example in the first scene, the pompous Ducie tries scene to teach the uninterested pupil about that anachonism, "*the mystery of sex*", and the consequence is a complex mixture of comedy and tragedy more of pathos. The double-edged satire of Forster is not so much present in *Maurice* except in scenes like this which makes somewhat a different novel altogether. As a homosexual tract, the novel has got some serious points to make still, Forster manages here to combine a serious critique of the Victorian approach to sexual education with some humourfilled dialogue. "One must not make a mystery of it. Then come the great things– *Love, Life*", pontificates Ducie, "All right with the world. Male and female! Ah wonderful!". One can see "the exhortations to be patriotic, athletic, learned and religious, that flowed like a four-part figure from Pembroke's mouth" in *The longest Journey*. The subject matter has changed from *esprit de corps to sex*, but the satire is still on the teaching method.

To understand the serioius side of this opening scene of *Maurice*, one must compare it with a similar scene in *Goldsworthy Lowers Dickinson*. Forster writes in this biography about Goldie never hearing one sensible word from any grown up person on the subject of sex. A "Pompous fattish man" named Earnest Coleridge taught him at his first school, and insisted on explaining "the mystery of sex". Forster writes:

> Later on, hearing that he had a
> bath with another boy, he called
> him to his study and cross-questioned
> him.

According to Forster, this incident was only one in many. Goldie's education made him a confused and repressed person. Impositiion of such flawed morality harmed him like *Maurice* he got really confused by "*vague and alarming sex talk*". Writes Forster:

> He became more devout
> ...Liking to feel good, and
> Sometimes longing to be bad.
> He was in a complete muddle
> Without any standards except
> What were imposed from outside
> and even his rebellions were
> conventional.

Maurice also suffers from "trance" is similarly muddled like Goldie, because of being a student at a public school. Like Goldie, he is good and bad by turns: he is "religious" and "obscene" Maurice is different from Goldie due to his physical strength as he is capable of defending himself. But, he is similarly vulnerable like Goldie. Of *Maurice*, Forster writes:

> The boys had showered presents on him,
> declaring he was brave. A great mistake,
> he wasn't brave: he was afraid of the dark.

Maurice although popular is mentally antagonised by school. Goldie Dickinson's situation perfectly encapsulates *Maurice's* mental trauma:

> **Goldie was not normal. He suffered from torments which assail the spirit, from moral bullying, of which there was a great deal, and from his own timidity.**

The dissatisfied protagonists of where *Angels fear to Tread* and *The longest Journey* also find their school days ennervating and painful. Same as *Maurice*, they "receive upon undefended the first blows of the world." Rickie considers his schooldays as "a hell no grown up devil can devise." due to the cruelty of his fellow students; similarly Philip has also miserable experiences because of his "Weakly build." For the boys, it is more of a spiritual torment rather than the confrntation with the bullies. Confirmity, a mechanical adherence to conventions, stifles individuality and creativity in the school. Forster depicts. Pembroke, for example, teaches that "Without innumerable customs, there is no safety, either for boys or men."

Confused to syches are very much present in the early novels and *Maurice* is also one of the case. Forster talks also about public school education in "Notes on the English character" He says :

> **A public school education does not make for mental clearness and the (Englishman) possesses to a very high degree the power of confusing his own mind.**

Forster depicts the problem of "undeveloped heart" in sketch of Philip in **Where Angels fear to Tread:**

His face was plain rather than not,
and there was a curious mixture
in it of good and bad… but below the
the nose and eyes all was confusion
and those people who believe that
destiny resides in the mouth shook
their heads when they looked at him.

So, for the author public school system's repressive methods leads to spiritual muddledom. Rickie, for example, creeps out of an enormous public school "Cold and friendless and ignorant...preparing for a silent journey." Maurice suffers from this spiritual muddledom in terms of his lack of a sexual identity. For years, after the unsufferable instructions of Ducie, he remains hopelessly "bewildered" about his homosexual temperament. These characters suffer from sexual frustration because of the boarding school system leading to violent form of rebellion:

If you need together human beings before
they can understand each other the
great god Pan is angry and will in
the end evade your regulations

A deeper exploration of the novels reveal how that family unit is one of the major symbols of society's oppression of the individual. Herrinton echoes Forster's views when she says :

All a child's life depends on the ideal
it has of its parents...Destroy that,
and everything goes...morals, behaviour,
everything.

By the practice of conventional morality, parents often perpetuate an unconsidered adherence to rigid set of values. In *Angels*, Philip's whole life is influenced by his mother. In *Journey*,

Rickie's early relations with his parents have a pronounced effect on his subsequent development. In *Maurice*, Forster depicts the hero's youth in a way which is reminiscent of a psychological case study. Wilfred Stone writes:

Never were children more cruelly

Suffocated by morality and over

Privilege than the poor little rich children of Forster's class and generation.

In Marianne *Thornton*, Forster coolly discusses the drawbacks of his own upbringing. According to his own account, he lost his father at an early age, and took up residence with his mother, "Aunt Monie" (Thornton), and other aunts. As a chile, he was molly-coddled: he was forced to play "eggy peggy", and compelled to wear "corkscrew curls". His aunt was whimsical and domineering, which made him unable to assert himself. Marianne although loved him enough to leave 8,000 pounds for him, unfortunately her love was suffocating. Forster took to writing when little "Long shories about-things that have never happened except inside (his) head". As he grew up, he transformed his childhood tensions into materials for creative fiction.

In *Angels*, *Journey*, *Room* with a view and *Maurice* Forster portrays the generation gap and the resultant struggles because of that. In all the novels, a young person has to fight against the conventional authority. Thus, the familial guidance provided for these characters is misleading. Smothering and destructive, inhibited and inhibiting by turns, it blocks the path to full development. Forster's sympathy lies with those people who cannot rebel; he feels the limitations with them placed upon an early growth. However, he keeps his admiration for those who express their own nature, even when this involves sudden and radical form of protest, Forster's first two heroes do not succeed in finding happiness for themselves. Despite their qualities, they ultimately prove too weak to vanquish their moral and sexual confusion. Compared to these two, Lucy Honeychurch and Maurice Hall rebel, thereby discovering new ways of living and loving according to their needs. Like Philip and Rickie, they are confined by their families, and by conventional morality, but eventually, they resolve the inner conflicts that threaten to destroy them.

In a novel like *Maurice*, Forster finally allows himself to give his complete attention to a family situation that interests him greatly. Thus, the first two chapters of this novel consist entirely of descriptions of *Maurice's* early experiences as the only son in a housefull of women. The first few pages points out the spiritual impoverishment that results from insisting a son to be exact copy of his dead father. His mother, Dr Barry, his teachers, and other authorities ask him to imitate his father in every way. He is sent to Maurice Hall's old public school, and is supposed to enter the stock exchange, to carry on the family tradition. For who is already pining for the garden boy, and vaguely anticipating that he will never marry, the worst edict involves marriage. The platitudinous Dr Barry pains *Maurice* deeply with his idle banter:

> **Who will present the expectant world**
> **with a *Maurice* the third? After which**
> **old age, grandchildren and finally the**
> **daisies.**

He transforms his thoughts into the form of inflexible commandments that scare the young boy. Says he:

> **Man that is born of woman must go with**
> **woman if the human race is to continue**

With these and other examples in which society makes parental authority a stultifying divinity for innocent children to worship, Forster adds one more feather in his critique of conventional morality.

More than the deceased father, it is Maurice's mother who turns out to be suffocating parent. Hall is yet another bored housewife in a bourgeois community.

> Church was the only place Hall
> had to go to the shops delivered...
> It was a land of facilities where
> nothing had to be striven for,
> and success was indistinguishable
> from failure.

Hall, who has very few duties and not much recreation, easily finds her place within the canon of Forsterian women. Like Elliott, Herriton and other mothers in his novels, she is the mistress of the house and must rest content with the shred of power this afferds her. As she has no husband, she completely devotes her life to her son. In the early years, "*Maurice* liked his home," Forster tells us,. "and recognised his mother as its presiding genius." As he is growing into a teenager however, her "very softness" angers him. He thinks.

> It cost her nothiing to muck about with
> tender words and toast: she only wanted
> to make him soft too.

Gradually, he realises that even their early affection for one another was harmful, since it involved an abnormal mother fixation. In one scene, the fifteen years old *Maurice* returns from school. Forster writes:

> They went kissing one another and
> conversing aimlessly.
> 'Morrie...',

'Mummie...'

'Now I must give my Morrie a lovely time.

This episode shows *Maurice* regression to infancy, because of his mother's abnormal obsession with him. One is reminded about Elliot who offers Rickie a great coat on his fifteenth birthday, and of Forster's own childhood position as the curly-haired "Important one" in *Marianne Thornton*. In all these instances, the affections of the mothers are twisted and misdirected.

Maurice shows us the frightening consequences of mother fixation. After his meeting with Durham in Cambridge, *Maurice* comes home for better :

> One strong feeling arouses another, and a profound irritation against his womankind set in. His relations with them had hitherto been trivial but stable, but it seemed iniquitous that anyone should mispronounce the name of the man who was more to him than all the world. Home emasculated everything.

Maurice is similar to the novel A *Room with a View* as once again, the beloved can be gained only by rejecting one's parents. However, here the theme gains much greater and more bitter emphasis. As *Maurice* is growing up, his family limits him in continually more serious ways. He must reject education system, religion and marriage, the basic institution at cambridge, Maurice rebels against authority, and starts thinking about himself. However, each family visit makes him regress more into confusion:

> Three weeks in their company, left
> him untidy, sloppy, victorions
> in every item, yet defeated on the
> whole. He came back to cambridge
> thinking, and even speaking, like
> his mother or Ada.

His female relatives plant a suburban soul in Maurice, and a repulsion for the opposite sex. Like Philip, he becomes angry when surrounded by too many females, Forster writes:

> They sat round the breakfast table, in
> morning because of grandpa, but otherwise
> worldly. Besides his mother and sisters,
> there was impossible Aunt Ida, who lived
> with them now, and a Tonks, a friend
> whom kitty had made...

Clearly, *Maurice* lacks from male companionship, he frets nervously about the possibility of marrying the unappealing Tonks, and his frustration intensifies.

As compared to *Maurice*, Clive Durham has enough intelligence to understand his relation with his mother long before *Maurice* has drawn any conclusion about him. Forster elaborates on the theme of familial relationship by depicting Clive as mortily-coddled aesthetile and his shrewd mother like Philip Herriton in *Where Angels Fear to Tread*, Clive detects his mother's unsincerity, and yearns to rebel. In the beginning of his friendship with Maurice, he admits to his hatred of Durham :

> I just have been pretending to like her.
> This row has shattered my lie. I did
> think I had stopped building lies. I

> despise her character, I am disgusted
> with her.

In a quarrel resembling those of Philip and Herriton, Clive decides his mother "Withered, unsympathetic, empty." In reality, she is a manipulative and worldly woman. As Herriton plans to recapture Lilia' baby, Clive's mother is a scheming woman who devises ways to find eligible match for her son:

> Durham had her motives. She was looking out wives for Clive, and put down the Hall girls on her list. She had a theory one ought to cross breeds a bit, and Ada, though suburban, was healthy...Durham did not propose to return to the dower house in practice, whatever she might do in theory and believed she could best manage Clive through his wife.

With such words, Forster vividly suggests this woman's arrogance and bossiness. One can sense how she is an important addition to already large group of unpleasant mother figures in Forster's fiction.

Chapter 3

Struggle for Happiness

Wilfred Stone defines fantasy in Forster's short stories as :

> ...a psychological phenomenon, as a means of getting. via dream, imagination, or wishful thinking what one cannot get in reality...The motive forces of fantasies are unsatisfied wishes, and every single fantasy is the fulfillment of a wish, a correction of unsatisfied reality...

In *Maurice* and Forster's early novels, fantasy is one of the devices the central protagonists employ in order to escape from the repressive existence. Philip, Rickie, Lucy and Maurice get alienated from themselves and their surrounding. Due to a conflict between their needs and the commands of their family, each becomes confused and trapped. Thus, they unconsciously attempt to escape from problems they have not visualised clearly. They are filled with unsatisfied desires, they frequently dream, travel or pursue various aesthetic and religious ideals. Only Maurice and Lucy go beyond distractions to find alternative solutions to their beredom and loneliness. Unfortunately for philip and fulfillment, no beloved comes to lead him to freedom and fulfillment. Despite varied endings of these novels, however, the potrayal of the struggle for happiness is very similar in each case, and a proper analysis is required to this quest.

Philip's departure from England in where *Angels Fear to Tread* gives him an opportunity to explore repressed desires. Forster utilises a twentieth century technique as he trans for Italy into a land where in reality is more like nighmare: reflecting his study of the unconscious wilfred Stone writes.

> For the last century and a half, such northern Europeans as Goethe, Arnold, Butler, Lawrence and Mann have in their writings made Italy a powerful symbol for release from repression, for all the sensuous and passionate side of life that restraints have made illicit.

Philip's visits to Italy represents an ephemeral plunge into the realm of fantasy. After each visit, he has to return to his suffocating existence in Sawston. Still, whenever he is away, he is able to release his bottled up emotion thereby achieving a small amount of satisfaction. Forster conteasts Sawston, "the realm of common sense," with Monteriaro, "a fantastic ship city of a dream." The moment Philip arrives, he fells into a sort of trance : "the sheer force of his intellect is weakened by the sight of Monteriano." Clearly, he enters into the land of sensuality and wish-fulfillment.

In addition to escaping from reality by cultivating his aesthetic sense (his sense of beauty), and burying himself in a useless legal career, he develops a sense of humour. Philip remains a complacent hero throughout his life. His attempts to rescue Gino baby is filled with lack of enthusiasm the same way he took up legal profession. Caroline gives voice to some of Forster's own exasperation with his ineffectual hero when she comments:

> Settle which side you'll fight on...Oh, what is the use of fair mindedness if you never decide for yourself ? Any one gets hold of you and makes you do what they want. And you see through them and

> laugh at them-and do it. If is not enough
> to see elearly... he must intend to accomplish
> not sit intending on a chair...You appreciate
> us all-see good in all of us. And all the
> time you are dead-dead-dead.

The vitality of Gino Carella is in direct contrast to the "deadness" of Philip, throughout the novel. Gino is symbolic of Forsterian virility, as he is both creative and destructive, violent and loving. On the one hand, he wants to create life:

> His one desise was to became the father
> of a man like himself...falling in love
> was a mere physical frivality...

On the other hand, he longs to destroy it. During the first meal, Philip was at Gino's home, the latter's cruelty is revealed:

> A Starved cat had been worrying them all
> ...Signor Carella...caught her by the paw
> and flung her away from him.

Later, it is revealed that he abuses his own wife, who responds with the gesture of a wounded animal. Philip likes both the cruelty and the beauty of Gino's nature. At first, he considers cino to be unsavoury but soon discovers the Italian's charm:

> The youth was hungry...And Philip had
> Seen that face before in Italy a hundred
> times-seen it and loved it...

Forster in *The life to come*, wrote a story, where a character who, like Gino, "loved to take life, as all those do who are really in touch with nature." Like the Gamekeeper, Alec Scudder of Maurice, Gino is a creature of the open air. Italian soil gives Gino a carefree existence. Gino welcomes Philip into his loggia, and into "the brotherhood of man is a reality." It is, in fact, a beautiful paradise for men only :

Italy is such a beautiful place if

You happen to be a man.

In Maurice, we see how Italy had adopted the code Napoleo by the Edwardian period. "There homosexuality is no longer crime", Maurice's hypontist advises him. Evidently, the Italian society depicted in *Where Angels fear to Tread* is more of a heaven for homosexuals since it excludes women and exalts men. This environment brings out Philip's love for men, as one night at the opera, he becomes 'drunk with excitement':

He deserted his ladies and plunged towards

the box...then his own hands were

seized affectionately. It all seemed

quite natural.

The hand, of course, belongs to Gino, and in a rare burst of spontaneity, Philip cavorts with this Italian and his group of friends. Philip feels intoxicated to the extreme:

Again he would be enchanted by the kind,

Cheerful voices, the laughter that was

Never vapid, the laughter that was

Of the arm across his back.

Bonding with Gino develops Philip's impoverished heart which he had brought from Sawstor. In a dramatic scene, Philip confronts the Italian with the sad story of the child's death. The nature of relationship between two men is revealed more fully than earlier: it has all the elements of physical torture, sexual attraction and idealism. Philip's feelings for Gino are more amorous than his response to Caroline. His brawl with the Italian provides him with a rare chance for physical contact, as well as the release of pent up emotions, ranging from pity and tenderness, to hatred and remorse. Philip feels bound to Gino by "ties of almost alarming intimacy." When Caroline admits the strength of her own feelings for Gino, Philip hears himself spontaneously remark: "Rather! I love him too." Back in England, Philip will have his only dreams, his aesthetic sentiments, and his memories of Gino to comfort him.

Rickie's Elliott of *The Longest Journey* is a hero of much the same mould. Like Philip, he must lead a highly active intellectual life in order to compensate for unsatisfactory aspects of his actual existence. From a very early age, he too must 'get via dream, imagination, or wishful thinking what he cannot get in reality.' Like Philip, Rickie is rarely aroused sexually, or capable of actualizing his passions. He, too, prefers to remain a viewer of life whenever possible.

The epigraph of *The Longest Journey* provides a clue as to how Rickie should spend his life. "Fratribus" is, in fact, the novel's major theme. At Cambridge, Rickie, Ansell and their friends enjoy a comradeship akin to that of Philip and Gino in Italy. This environment develops Rickie's lovely personality.

> In one year, he had made many friends
> and learnt much, and he might learn
> even more...

In Goldworthy Lowes Dickinson, he evokes the spirit of the school:

> As Cambridge filled up with friends it
> acquired a magic quality. Body and
> spirit, reason and emotion, work and
> play, architecture and scenery, laughter
> and seriousness, life and art-these
> pairs which are contrasted elsewhere

> were there fused into one-peope and
> books reinforced one another, intelligence
> joined hands with affection, Speculation
> became a passion and discussion was
> made profound by love.

Rickie's stay at Cambridge possesses much of this magic quality. Thus, the novel begins with a scene of undergraduate bliss. Like Philip, Rickie considers his first whiff of freedom and stimulation intoxicating. The boys simply sit in their rooms, light matches, sip tea, and discuss philosophical issues; the aura of insouciance and masculine informality surrounding their gathering parallels that of Gino world, and of Clouds Hill. One remembers Forster's depiction of the "happy casualness" of clouds hill, where "there were no fixed hours for meals and no one sat down." Despite this casual atmosphere, these societies are highly exclusive. Cloud shill and Fraternal Italy excludes all women; the brotherhood of Cambridge excludes women. The featernity of cambridge recalls Forster's dream of "aristocracy of the sensitive, the considerate and plucky." Thus, when Agnes enters the room, the boys run "like mists before the sun," and Ansell refuses to acknowledge her existence.

Just as Philip finds Gino in Italy, Rickie discover Stuart Ansell at college. This male bonding proves to be one of the most satisfactory experiences of his life. Ansell, with his Bloomsburian standards, conscientiously teaches his friend about the values of truth and affection. Like Maurice and Clive, however, these boys suffer because of the unconventionality of their relationship. Rickie dreams of public sanction for his private acts as he wished there was a "friendship office where the marriage of true minds could be registered". Just as Philip's friendship with Gino functions only in Italy, so Rickie and Ansell can be together freely only in the isolation of Cambridge.

One of the passage in the novel sounds surprising like Maurice, Rickie thinks:

> Nature has no use for us: she has cut her staff differently. Dutiful sons, Loving husbands, responsible Father-these are what she wants, and if we are friends, it must be in our spare time...a few scraps of poetry is all that survives of David and Jonathan.

When Rickie acts according to his wishes, he and Ansell Cavort like lovers. together in a meadow, the two boys resemble Maurice and Clive on a Cambridge spree

> 'Don't go', Ansell said Idly. 'It is much better for you to talk to me'.
> 'Lemme go, Stewart'.
> You-simply-can't get away. I wish I wanted to bully you.'

Rickie laughed, and over-balanced suddenly in the grass Ansell, with unusual playfulness, held him prisoner. They lay there for a few minutes, talking and ragging aimlessly.

Frederick Crew talks about this scenc:

> Rickie, Strictly speaking, is not a homosexual , but his physical handicap and his effeminary are such that the more genuine strains of homosexuality in Ansell strikes a more responsible chord in him.

We do not know for certain whether Rickie is homosexual or not, he is indeed a lover of friendship rather than marriage. In

Cambridge, he likes a passage from Shelly's Epipsychidion, where in the prison like aspect of marriage is talked about. This poem provides the novel with its title, and Rickie with the seeds of philosophy:

> 'I never was attached to that great sect,
> Whose doctrine is that each one should
> select out of the world a mistress or a friend,
> and all the rest, though fair and wise,
> commend to cold oblivion,–though it is the
> code of modern morals, and the beaten
> road which those poor slaves with weary
> footsteps tread who travel to their home
> among the dead by the broad highway of
> the world,–so with one sad friend, perhaps
> a jealous foe, The dreariest and the longest
> journey go.'

Instead of marrying, Rickie feels he should "love everyone equally." Ansell, who is potrayed as homosexual scoff at the decision to love all mankind, but he is appreciative of his friend's decision not to marry.

Of course, Rickie changes his mind about marriage, and proposes to Agnes Pembroke. However, in his potrayal of Rickie's marriage, he potrays the latent horrors of wedlock, for those who are unsuited. The deformed, lame child who is born out of this wedlock is an emblem of to it mutual failure, and Rickie vows to pay heed to "the lesson he had learnt glibly so at Cambridge...; no child should ever be born to him again."

When compared to the tremulous physicality of Ansell and Rickie at Cambridge, the relationship of Agnes and Rickie seem barren despite the fact they have a child together. Like Clive's wife in Maurice, or Rickie's own mother, Agnes is reticent:

Rickie valued emotion...become it is
the only final path to intimacy.
she, ever robust and practical,
always discouraged him. She was
not cold; She would willingly
embrace him. But she hated being
upset, and would laugh or thrust
him off when his voice grew serious.

Soon, the married couple have no topic for conversation. Forster writes:

The tone of their marriage
life was soon set. It was to be
a frank good-fellowship, and before
long Rickie found it difficult to
speak in a deeper key.

Agnes effectively cuts Rickie off from the stimulating dialogue he shared with Ansell as a Cambridge undergraduate, and jealousy prevents any of his efforts to maintain contact with his old friend. Rickie soon becomes a prisoner of spiritual wasteland, and the grim aspects of marriage depicted in Shelly's poem are fully realised.

Throughout the courtship and marriage of Rickie and Agnes, Ansell warns his friend constantly of the dangers of relationship. Crews is right in assuming that Ansell is a homosexual. For example, his protest at the itme of betrothal is sinular to those of a jealous suitor. Rickie's situation at this time is comparable to that of live Durham in *Maurice*. In both cases, a male. The series of letters he writes indicates the intensity of his feelings, and Rickie responds with an equal excitement. Even in the midst of his own happiness with Agnes, he writes to his friend:

> This letter of yours is the most
> wonderful thing that has ever
> happened to me yet–more wonderful
> (I do not exaggerate) than the moment
> when Agnes promised to marry me...
> you have written to me, "I hate the
> woman who will be your wife," and
> I write back, "hate her. Can't
> I love you both?"

The reality is that Rickie cannot love them both, and Ansell becomes more and more miserable becuase of this truth. He sublimates his feelings to a hatred of all females, and the word "Lady Like" becomes insult on his Lips. According to him, women cannot be comrades as he says :

> 'Men and women desire different things
> Man wants to love mankind; woman wants
> to love one man. When she has him her
> work is over. She is the emissary of
> Nature, and Nature's bidding has been
> fulfilled. But man does not care a damn
> for Nature–or at least only a very little
> damn...'

With these declarations, Ansell joins a long line of Forsterian misogynists, many of whom are inclined homosexually.

In the characterisation of Stephen Wonham, Forster links the themes of paganism and comradeship, (This particular association of ideas is very common in the writings of Edward Carpenter, the ideologist of homosexuality and democracy.) Stephen's room is constructed on classical lines, and a picture of the Demeter is its only decoration. Ansell also summarises Stephen's character:

Certain figures of the Creek, to
whom we continually return,
suggested him a little. One
expected nothing of him...
–Yet the conviction grew that
he had been back somewhere
back to some table of the
gods, spread in a field where
there is no noise, and that he
belonged forever to the guests
with whom he had eaten.

Stephen extends the hand of friendship to Rickie in earnest. Far from the sterility of Sawston, the two men stand together for a moment in a world of their own creation :

The suburb was now wrapped
in a cloud, not of its own
making. Sigh after sigh
passed along its streets to
break against dripping walls.
The schools, the houses were
hidden, and all civilization
seemed in abeyance. Only the
simplest sounds, the simplest
desires emerged.

Stephen beckons to Rickie in freshly-minted words of love :

'Come with me as a man', said Stephen,
already out in the mist. 'Not as a

> brother, who cares what people did
> years back ? We're alive together,
> and the rest is cant. Here am I,
> Rickie, and there are you...Come,
> I do mean it. Come, I will take
> care of you, I can manage you.'

Rickie accepts Stephen's invitation, and the two men depart at sunset. Their mood parallels that of Maurice and Alex at the conclusion of *Maurice*. Unlike Maurice, Rickie's desires are not fulfilled. He dies, saving his friend's life, as well as his own soul: but earthly joys will never be his.

Questions about salvation of the soul ring loud and clear in each of Forster's novels. As intelligent reader our field of analysis should now shift to Lucy and Maurice, two forsterian protagonists, who live happily ever after, and save their souls as well, Unlike Rickie and Philip, these two characters are satisfied by the conclusion of their respective stories.

In *A Room with a view*, Forster depicts again the Italian setting of *Where Angels fear to Tread*, and once again uses it to symbolise a place, where unconscious desires can be explored. As she wanders through the strats of Florence she begins to feel restless for the first time in her life. However, she still cannot recognise the exact nature of her desires :

> 'The world', she thought, 'is certainly
> full of beautiful things, if only I
> could come across them.'

Forster subtly hints at Lucy wanting sex, by making use of the same phallicimagery he used in *Where Angels fear to Tread* :

> Lucy desired more...she fixed her
> eyes wistfully on the tower of the
> palace, which rose out of the

lower darkness like a pillar
of roughened gold. It seemed
no longer a tower, no longer
supported by earth, but some
unattainable treasure throbbing
in the tranquil sky.

Lucy represses her feelings for George, which makes her lose out her balance. Like Rickie and Maurice, she becomes played by night mares, and visions of ghosts in the dark. At times, she despairs of controlling her feelings at all :

How would she fight against ghosts ?
for a moment the visible world
faded away, and memories and emotions
alone seemed real.

A Room with a view resembles Forster's other novels, in that both the negative and postitive aspects of possessing an artistic temperament are presented. As usual, Forster emphasises the dangers of a complete withdrawal into an aesthetic haven. Lucy's beauty and musical talent attracts the attention of Cecil Yse. Like Philip and Rickie, Cecil transfigures people into works of art.

In this happiest depsetion of Forster's novels, Lucy does, of course, eventually comes to her senses, and breaks her engagement off to the unsuitable Cecil. However, she keeps on deceiving herself for sometime and her life loses its meaning. Forster writes:

She gave up trying to
understand herself, and
joined the vast armies of
the benighted, who follow
neither the heart nor the
brain, and march to their
destiny by catch words.

Like Philip, Rickie, or Maurice, Lucy decides to busy herself in hard work. As an Edwardian woman, she cannot easily become a lawyer, a teacher, or a stock broker; thus, she dedicates herself to womanhood itself. Frustration makes her determined to become emancipated :

> **She must be one of the women**
> **whom she had praised so**
> **eloquently, who care for**
> **liberty and not for men.**

Paradoxically, the "Women's Liberation Movement" becomes imprisonment in Lucy's case, since her heart prompts her to marry George instead. "I might even share a flat for a little with some other girl", She tells her mother, obstinately denying her true feelings.

In contrast with Lucy's attempts to marry the respectable but limited Cecil, or to settle down to a career, she does not want, stands her ever growing relationship with the Emersons. The two men represent precisely the form of comradeship Forster's own soul yearned for democratic, unconventional, and at home approach in the open air, they reveal continually that they are capable of spontaneous gesture of affection towards the world, and each other.

The Reverend Beebe, one of the most intriguing characters in Forster's fiction, also like the unpopular Emersons. Like lucy, he repeatedly champions their cause. In an araticle entitled "The Homosexual theme in *A Room with a view*", Jeffrey Meyers says :

> **Beebe's latent homosexuality has**
> **been released and he has fallen**
> **in love with George.**

However, the novel offers a different explanation than Meyers. As Lucy's engagement to Cecil breaks off, Beebe rejoices. Forster writes :

His belief in celibacy, so reticent,

so carefully concealed beneath his

tolerance and culture, now came

to the surface and extended like

some delicate flower. 'They that marry do well, but they that refrain do better

In other words, a Christian belief in chastity motivates this well-intentioned rector. Nonetheless, Meyers is right in considering. *A Room With a view* having homosexual overtones. Looking at the chapter-12 of the novel, most readers of *Maurice* and *The life to come and other stories* can make sense of the interlocking themes of brotherhood and homosexuality. Just as Gino has called to Philip, or Stephen to Rickie, so, too, Freddy impetuously asks his male companions to steal away with him. 'How d'ye do? Come and have a bathe.' Part of the Pleasure arises from leaving the ladies behind. Once again, Forster suggests that marriage all too often, is merely an enforced 'long journey', and that less possessive male bonding can be a better alternative. The three men certainly partake of this pleasurable combination of emotions, as they swim and play in the lovely pool. As they shed their clothes, they abandon the restrictive atmosphere of laws and convention. However, one can see in *A Room with a View*, he affirms the value of both George's romp in the pool with the men, and his eventual marriage. As for Lucy, according to Mr. Emerson, she must marry, or her life will be wasted. Only through George will she find "the tenderness, and the comradeship, and the poetry" for which she yearns. The novel's conclusion shows Mr. Emerson's prophecy being fulfilled.

Clearly, Lucy's tendency towards sublimating her passions to dream, art, religion, or hard work has subsided, and her married life holds the promise of considerable happiness.

Maurice charts a central character's progress from an existence based on wish-fulfilling fantasies to one rooted in the love of another person. In his first school, Maurice pretends to be an average schoolboy-bully, who likes dominating boys weaker than him, and becomes popular for his "bravery". This illusion of stength is his first source of comfort. His own home scares him as he feels lonely, confused there. Like Rickie, at the age of fourteen, Maurice cries abnormally at the slightest provocation. He suffers from "childish collapses" into hysteria due to the inner conflict just swelling within him. Rickie, as we see, desires a brother at times like these; Maurice cries for a garden boy named George, and becomes more miserable. Forster, was a nervous youngstertoo: "I was not a bad child but could be hysterical, pretentious, and detestable." cf, E.M. Forster, *Marianne Thornton : A Domestic Biography* (New York : Harcourt, Brace and Co., 1956, p. 305.). These unsolicited desires bother Rickie and Maurice throughout their childhood. They are particular, present at night, which accounts for the fact that they both were afraid of the dark as children.

During sleep, repressed desires come to the surfac. Forster believed that dreams represent some of our innermost thoughts. In *Maurice*, he writes :

Where all is obscure and unrealised
the best similitude is a dream.

Supernatural monsters destroy the slumber of Rickie and Maurice. Rickie cries for his mother to kill a "ghost in the passage," and Maurice Hall imagines that he sees "blots like skulls falling over the furniture." Maurice's looking glass and the street lamp outside his window casts eerie shadows. He does not call his mother; instead, he whispers "George, George", and the phantom disappears paradoxically.

> The second dream is more difficult
> to convey. Nothing happened. He scarcely
> saw a face, scarcely heard a voice say,
> "that is your friend", him with beauty and
> over, having filled" him with beauty
> and tenderness. He could die for
> such a friend, he would allow such
> a friend to die for him; they
> would make any sacrifice for each
> other, and count the world nothing,
> neither death nor distance nor
> crossness would part them, because
> "this is my friend"...

The naked body of George in the first dream referred to above represents unrestrained physical passion. Maurice's yearnings for a male lover fill him with the guilt he cannot understand, and his "resentment" in the dream mirrors his actual reaction, When the garden boy quits the job. The second dream shows a spiritual love. As contrary to the naked body of the lover in the earlier dream, the second image contains "scarcely...a face, scarcely...voice". "brutal disappointment" is replaced by a feeling of "beauty and tenderness". Here, Maurice craves for an ideal friend, and one is reminded of the belief that through the love of one person, one can love God. He thinks of Christ, and a "Greek god, such as illustrated the classical dictionary". Clearly, he longs for perfection. His thinking about the beloved resembles religious worship : he expresses a willingness to sacrifice himself and "count the world nothing", if it proves necessary. As the novel unfolds, Maurice lives out the prophecies in these powerfulk, obscure images from his "secret life". When he loves Clive, he experiences the anger, guilt and frustration of the first dream, in loving Alec Scudder, he experiences the tranquil ecstasies symbolized by the second dream. Forster tells us :

> **Maurice's secret life can be understood**
> **now; it was palt brutal, part ideal,**
> **like his dreams.**

Maurice's dreams follow a curious pattern found throughout Forster's fiction; whenever a potentially sexual relationship is curbed, there emerges a combination of physical torture, attraction, and idealism that is amply reflected in Maurice's fantasies. In *Where Angels Fear to Tread*, one could witness, Gino simultaneously being cruel and beautiful, filling Philip with both contempt and tenderness. Simlarly, in *The Longest Journey*, Rickie Elliotts friendship with both Gerald Dawes and Stephen Wonham "the bully...who knocks one down", partake of this mixture of emotions. For example, at public school, Rickie is exposed to Gerald's brutality. Forster carefully chronicles the tortures inflicted; Rickie suffers from "pinches, kicks, boxed ears, twisted arms, pulled hair, ghosts at night, inky books, befouled photographs". When both meet years later, Rickie hates Gerald, much as Maurice feels "cross" when he faces the fleeing football player of the first dream. This hatred, however soon turns into strong physical attraction. As Rickie stares at Gerald, he looks at his beauty longingly :

> **There stood a young man who**
> **had the figure of a Greek athlete**
> **and the face of an English one.**
> **He was fair and clean shaven,**

> and his colourless hair was
> cut rather short. The sun was
> in his eyes, and they, like his
> mouth, seemed scarcely more than
> slits in his healthy skin. Just
> where he began to be beautiful
> the clothes started. Round his
> neck went an up-and-down
> collar and a mauve-and-
> gold tie, and the rest of his
> limbs were hidden by a grey
> lounge suit, carefully creased
> in the right places.

Like Maurice in his dream, Rickie does not understand his feelings. He has a certain amount of guilty conscience just as Maurice feels his thoughts of George are "somehow a punishment for something"; so Rickie associates sensual desires with sin :

> He wondered whether after all...bodily
> beauty and stength were signs of
> the soul's damnation.

Soon, Rickie idealizes his reltionship with Gerald. *Maurice*, Rickie wants like to make sacrifices for the man, who has captured his affections. Thus, he gifts Gerald a large sum of money. (The close connection between Maurice's dreams and *The Longest Journey* becomes more apparent when we remember that Gerald, is a football player). Rickie's attempt to transcend ordinary reality is an immediate failure. "He muddles all day with poetry, and old, dead people", says Agnes, "and then tries to bring it into life". Gerald dies at this point suddenly in the narration, and Rickie's obscure desires remain unfulfilled.

Even Agnes's vicarious participation in Gerald's brutality indicates that in Forster's univers, both males and females, homosexuals and hetrosexuals enjoy this lethal combination of sex and violence. In *A Room with a view, Forster's* most heterosexual novel, this becomes increasingly clear. Lucy's first major meeting with George occurs on the Piazza Signoria twilight, while a man is being killed. This scene depicts forster's habitual approach to the theme of sexual repression. Lucy falls into George's arm in a swoon at this point of narration. Forster shows her fainting couched in sexual terms :

> **Even as she caught sight of him**
> **he grew dim; the palace itself grew**
> **dim, swayed above her, fell on to her**
> **softly, slowly, noiselessly, and the**
> **sky fell with it...George Emerson**
> **still looked at her, but not across**
> **anything. She had complained of**
> **dullness, and lo (lo)! one man was**
> **stabbed, and another held her**
> **in his arms.**

Lucy and George become sexually and spiritually aware of one another in this violent backdrop. As Lucy cannot accept her feelings, she sublimates them to thoughts about the brutality of the accident. She thinks about the photographs which have been splattered with blood. In her guilt, she asks George to forget the incident but her unconscious concern with her own sexuality emerges. As the scene ends, she hopes George will "avert his eyes from her nakedness like the knight in the beautiful picture."

From the brief analysis of Forster's theme of sexual repression, believe that Maurice's vivid noctural dream functions as comprehensive summary of what the author meant when he speaks of "brutality" and "idealism"–the two of his favourite subjects. Maurice's adolescent dreams are one of the most interesting features of the novel. However, one must turn other elements of Maurice's sublimated sexuality. Maurice tries to appease his desires in the same manner as Rickie, Philip, and Lucy although he has no idea about them. Maurice is different from such characters as he does not have artistic world to console. He does not like paintings, or writing stories or playing the piano. Forster, *Goldsworthy Lowers Dickenson,* p.15 : As a youth, Goldie finds his only satisfaction in "the world of Ariel". With the exception of Maurice, Forster's male heroes resemble Goldie in their love of art. The child like powers of vision that become the means of a vital imaginative life for Rickie and Philip evades him entirely, when he turns sixteen. Forster writes :

> He had lost the precocious
> clearness of the child which
> transfigures and explains the
> universe, offering answers
> of miraculous insight and
> beauty.

Thus, he is dependent on crude waking pleasures instead, although these will provide temporary meagre nourishment. (Several reviews of Maurice criticize Forster for the "thin writing" of the particular part of his work. One could presurre the author provides only the barest details of Maurice's early sexual life to emphasise over the intensity of young homosexual's frustration.

> He longed for smut...books : the
> school library was immaculate,
> but while he was at his grandfather's
> he came across an unexpurgated

martial...thoughts : he had a dirty
little collection. Acts : he desisted
from these after the novelty was
over...

Maurice loves his work unlike Philip and Rickie when he grows older, he becomes successful in the business world : Everyone thinks that he is "the right sort of stock-broker." However, he, has become too professional mechanically. After graduation, he joins his father's firm without any thought. Writes Forster, disapprovingly :

Maurice was stepping into
the niche that England
had prepared for him.

Maurice focuses totally on his work when he loses clive. He attempts to compensate for his loneliness by "setting himself to acquire new habits" and "practicing a severe self discipline," like the earlier characters.

Maurice resembles the earlier works, Forster is appreceative of his hero's competence and dedication. Maurice's work at this point in his development resembles Rickie's efforts to please angry gods over rejection of his brother. Both admirable and futile.

Forster comments :

Maurice was doing a fine thing-proving
on how little the soul can exist...He
hadn't a God, he hadn't a lover–the
two usual incentives to virtue. But on
he struggled with his back to ease
because dignity demanded it...struggles
like his are the supreme achievement
of humanity, and surpass any legends

> about heaven.
> No reward awaited him. This work,
> like much that had gone before,
> was to fall ruining.

Indeed, Maurice stands to die spiritual death akin to the of Rickie at Sawston school. He turns into a slave in an urban society that threatens to destroy his unrealised individuality forever. Maurice chooses to ignore his homosexuality and focuses on his career, which leads to the risk of complete Fossilization.

He Ponders :

> Indoors was his place and there he had
> moulder, a respectable pillar
> of society, who has never had the
> chance to misbehave.

Only through breaking with the tradition of his father and, in fact, with conventional morality, Maurice does manage to come alive. Forster in this novel depicts the clash of pleasure over duty, and chooses the freedom of the great outdoors, rather than the confines of city life, in his distinct manner. Like Scudder, who belongs to a family of tradesman, Maurice must Learn to become an "untamed son of the woods," instead of remaining an ambitious businessman in search of career "opening." The moment Maurice accepts his homosexuality, he perceives his entire milieu in a new light. Forster takes up this opportunity to present one of his most effective condemnations of his own class. He writes :

> The clientele of Messrs Hill and
> Hall was drawn from the middle
> –middle classes, whose highest
> desire seemed shelter-continuous

> shelter– ...everywhere and always, until the existence of earth and sky is forgotten, shelter from poverty and disease and violence and impoliteness; and consequently from joy...Maurice saw from their faces as from the faces of his clerks and his partners, that they had never known real joy. Society had catered for them too completely...

One wishes Maurice turns away from this bourgeois complacency as a sensitive reader.

Maurice resembles Forster's early novels most specifically in its handling of theme of comradeship. Maurice can escape from this alienating aspect of his life by only finding kndred spirits. Rickie becomes aware of other people while studying at cambridge:

> Once inside college his discoveries multiplied. People turns out to be alive...as he strolled through the courts at night...there came by no process of reason a conviction that they were human beings with feelings akin to his own.

Clive Durhan captures his attention, and friendship becomes his chief objective :

> To ascend, to stretch a hand up

the mountainside until a hand catches
it, it was the end for which he had
been born.

Clive and Maurice commune clandestinely in the fields, smoking pan-like pipes; they bathe in a pool as radiant as the sacred Lake of *A Room With a View.*

Forster, emphasises about the rarity of their relation, just as Philip is more honest in Italian language than his native tongue, Clive and Maurice are more authentic when they speak in the language they create for themselve Forster writes :

No tradition overawed the boys. No
convention settled what was
poetic, what absurd. They were
concerned with passion that a few
English minds have admitted
and so created untrammelled
something of exquiste beauty
arose in the mind of each at least,
something unforgettable and eternal...

Maurice's second relationship with Alec Scudder shows the final extension of typical Forsterian oppositon of comradeship and society.

Maurice yearns for freedom and companionship; feeling restricted over Clive's respectable country estate.

He moaned, half asleep
there was something better
than this rubbish, if only
he could get to it-love-
nobility-big spaces, where passion

> clasped peace, spaces no science
> could reach, but they existed
> for ever, full of woods some of
> them, and arched with majestic
> sky and a friend.

Maurice must "live outside class, without relations or money, in order to have under bliss." However, the temptations of society cannot compare with the ecstasy of companionship. Further the relationship between Maurice and Alec Scudder gets strengthened by the opposition of their enemies. "Only a struggle twists sentimentality and lust together into love", writes Forster. A game of cricket that "takes on the semblance of reality" presents the dynamics of battle to be fought by the united outcasts better than anything else in the novel:

> They played for the sake of
> each other and of their fragile
> relationship if one fell the other
> would follow. They intended no
> harm to the world, but so long
> as it attacked, they must punish,
> they must stand wary, then hit
> with full stength, they must show
> that when two are gathered
> together, majorities shall not
> friumph.

Forster truly thus makes us feel the true fellowship possible between men.

Chapter 4

Treatment of Sexuality

We shall analyse about the protagonists where we discover Philip, Rickie, Lucy and Maurice begin with "undeveloped hearts", and undergo parallel experiences that help them change. In *Howard's End,* Forster presents us with the character that has developed a heart. Margaret Schlegel responds maturely and honestly to under variety of situations. She is the most heroic Forsterian character, and is depicted in the following manner:

> Away she hurried, not beautiful, not
> supremely brilliant, but filled with
> something that took the place of
> both qualities–something that is
> best described as a profound
> vivacity, a continual and
> sincere response to all that
> she encountered in her path
> through life!

Margaret acts. she did not want to be manipulated even during her childhood:

> The Schlegels had been left motherless
> when Tibby was born, when Helen was five
> and Margaret herself but thirteen...Mrs.
> Munt could without impropriety offer
> to go and keep house at Wickham
> Place. But her brother-in-law...
> had referred the question to
> Margaret, who with the crudity

> of youth had answered, 'No!
> they could manage much better
> alone'.

Margaret decides to reject the surrogate motherhood of Aunt Juley Munt. This upper middle class matron is as snobbish and meddlesome as Herriton, Failing, or Durham. She says, listening to Helen's unexpected engagement :

> 'Margaret, if I may interfere,
> don't be taken by surprise
> What do you think of the
> Wilcoxes ? Are they our sort ?
> Are they likely people.

Mrs. Munt's life is empty like the other women of her category, She lends her services withingly to her niece.

> 'Dear, I have nothing to call
> me back to Swan age'. She spread
> out her plump arms. ' I am
> all at your disposal. Let
> me go down to this house whose
> name I forget, instead of you'

Margaret, very unwillingly, accepts her aunt's proposal. Her tolerable attitude towards her sister's action stands in direct contrast to Munt's conventional appraisal of the situation. Margaret thinks:

> If she herself shonld ever fall in
> love with a man, she like Helen,
> would proclaim it from the house
> but as she only loved a
> sister, she used the voiceless
> language of sympathy.

The Journey to Howards End proves to be disastrous. Munt's interference leads to destruction. Her complacent attitude towards life is revealed; when she returns to wickan place.

> She soon recovered...before
> many days were over she had
> forgotten the part played by
> her own impudence in the
> catastrophe.

Munt proves again to be catasteophe for Tibby Schlegel's life. He is not only the youngest member of his family, but its only surviving male like Maurice. He becomes an "important one", and is inappropriately babied. Schlegel sister's nostalgia about childhood days make them remember an "unsuccessful visit of Aunt Juley's when she did not realize that "Tibby had grown up." In her foolish way, she made the boy sing a childish song every day for three weeks. Finally, he threw a temper tantrum, much like those of Maurice and Rickie on similar occasions. Like these characters, Tibby is insulted and overprotected by turns. In the begining of the novel, he is "intelligent...but dyspeptic and difficult." He is independent like his sisters as he needs extra affection. This extra love is provided by Margaret, who is eight year senior to him. She acts like his surrogate mother when she nurses him through a bad bout of hay fever. Tubby's relationship with his sisters is thus not stable. Margaret "cannot bear her brother to be scolded." She tries to make peace between Helen and Tibby.

> It pleased Margaret to hear
> her brother and sister talking.
> they did not get an over well as
> a rule. For a few moments, she
> listened to them, feeling elderly
> and benign.

Helon is jealous of her brother's too much dependence on the older sister, in the same way Kitty and Adaas tired of hearing Hall coddling Maurice.

Occasionally, Margaret joins her sisters in making fun of Tibby. His carelessness and effeminate gestures irritate them. He warms a teapot "almost too deftly", sighs and wears his hair long. The girls cannot refrain from criticising him :

> 'All right, Aunt Tibby', called Helen.
> while Margaret, thoughtful again,
> said : 'In a way, I wish he had
> a real boy in the house–...?
> 'So do I', said her sister. 'Tibby
> cares only for cultured females
> singing Brahms.'

At other times, the sisters respect Tibby. They ask him for advice whenever they are in trouble, since he is, indeed, the man of their household. Helen's pregnancy makes both the sisters approach Tibby. Like Ada and Kitty, their feelings for their brother vacillate continually.

As for Tibby himself, like Philip Herriton and other Forsterian male characters, he has been overwhelmed by the women in his family. This suffocating atmosphere makes him rebellious. The Schlegel sisters have been so intensely concerned with personal reltionships that has dried up their brother's capability to love.

> He had never been interested
> in human beings, for which
> one must blame him, but
> he had rather too much of
> them at Wickham

> Place...ought Margaret to
> know what Helen Knew
> the Basts to Know? Similar
> questions had vexed him from
> infancy...

Tibby never learns to love when compared to Maurice, loving two men. Ultimately, he is more like Philip, Rickie, Cecil Vyse and Clive Ducham, as he escapes often into the world of thought and act. He is different from these characters in the sense that he does not have the fleeting consolation of comradeship. His college days does not make him aware about the beauty of friendship:

> His Oxford remained Oxford empty,
> and he took into life with him, not the memory of radiance,
> but the memory of a colour
> scheme.

Forster depicts Tibby's development of being irrevocably stunted. He is completely opposite to his passionate involved sisters :

> The years between eighteen
> and twenty two, so magical
> for most, were leading him
> gently from boyhood to
> middle age. He had never
> known young-manliness,
> that qualitiy which warms
> the heart till death...He was
> frigid, though no fault of his
> own, and without cruelty.

Tibby's coldness is the result of his mobility "to connect" The use of the word "frigid" Shows that he is both sexually and emotionally inadequate. This is a serious defect in the light of the novel's epigraph, indeed. Margaret Schlegel's personal belief embodies the central theme of *Howards End:*

> Only connect: That was the
> whole of her sermon. Only
> connect the prose and the
> passion, and both will be
> exalted, and human love will
> be seen at its height. Live
> in fragments no longer. Only
> connect, and the beast and
> the monk, robbed of the
> isolation that is life to
> either, will die.

The first bead in the exalted chain of connections envisaged by Margaret is sexuality. The "beast" symbolizes sex without love, and the "monk" represents prudery. Margaret's words are similar to Mr. Emerson's views in *A Room with a View* :

> Man has to pick up the use
> of his functions as he goes along
> –especially the function of love...
> I only wish poets would say
> this too : that love is of the
> body : not the body, but of the
> body. Ah! the misery that
> would be saved if he confessed
> that : Ah! for a little directness
> to liberate the soul :

Margaret and Mr. Emerson are mouthpieces of Forster when they talk about man's obligation to acknowledge sex. Bonnie Finkelstein defines Forster's thinking accurately when she writes :

Each person must accept
sexuality internally by connecting
his or her own 'beast' side
with his or her own 'monk'
side.

Lionel Trilling observes in his discussion of *Howard's End* :

The sexual theme plays
through the book, lightly,
without much pressure...
but with great seriousness.
The great fact about the
Wilcoxes is that which
D.H. Lawrence saw, the fact
of sexual deficiency.

The sexual lack is most visible in Henry Wilcox. Twice married and middle aged, he is as confused as the adolescent Maurice Hall. The following passage reminds one of the public school mentality defined in Forster's early novels :

Outwardly, Henry was cheerful,
reliable, and brave; but within,
all had reverted to chaos
ruled, as for as it was ruled
at all, by an incomplete
asceticism. Whether as a boy,
husband, or widower, he had

the sneaking belief always
that bodily passion is bad...

Like Maurice, Henry's beautiful face and figure invests him with an aura of strength and attractiveness. Forster tells us, that Margaret finds him appealing enough :

His Complexion was robust, his
hair had receded but not
thinned, the thick moustache
and the eyes that Helen had
compared to brandy- balls
has an agreeable menace
in them...

Only a closer inspection of his physiognomy exposes its symbolic weaknesses:

His face was not as square
as his son's and, indeed,
the chin, though firm in
outline, retreated a little,
and the lips, ambiguous, were
curtained by a moustache...

Henry's weak mouth is like Philip, of whose face Forster describes :

Below the nose and eyes all
was confusion, and those people
who belive that destiny resides
in the mouth and chin shook
their heads when they looked
at him.

His moustache, however, is not like Maurice's. The "Episode of Gladys Olcott" needs to be analysed:

> Now Maurice, though he did not know it, had become an attractive young man...He was heavy but alert, and his face seemed following the example of his body. Mrs. Hall put it down to his moustache- 'Maurice's moustache will be the making of him'–a remark more profound than she has realised. Certainly the little black line of it did pull his face together and show up his teeth when he smiled...
>
> He turned his smile on Miss Olcott –it seemed the proper thing to do ...he pressed her little hand between his own...His touch revolted her. It was a corpse's

Not only this scene sheds light on Maurice's deeply–rooted homosexuality, it also shows how he is capable of mechanical and inappropriate sexual gestures. This scene also foreshadows Clive's prudish kissing of Maurice, on his later visit of Forster, Maurice p.153. This scene recalls Henry Wilcox's ineffec trial mode of kissing Margaret :

> She was startled, and nearly screamed, but recovered herself at once...on Looking back, the

> incident displeased her. It
> was so isolated. Nothing in
> their previous conversation
> had hearalded it, and worse
> still, no tenderness had ensued.

Henry's kiss reveals his arbitrary quality of sensuality, it is more of a kiss of a "beast" rather than that of a loving man. For Forster, a failure to connect sexually results in lack of self–awareness. If one considers sexuality as primary link in the chain of connections, then self–identify becomes the second link. Forster comments by presenting Hency Wilcox's sexual bewilderment :

> It was hard going in the roads
> of Mr. Eilcox's soul. From boyhood
> he had neglected them. 'I am not
> a fellow who bothers about my
> own inside.'

As Mr. Wilcox does not understand his own psyche he represents modern man. Forster writes :

> But man is an odd, sad creature as
> yet, intent on pilfering the earth,
> and heedless of the growth within
> himself. He cannot be bored about
> psychology. He leaves it to the
> specialist, which is as if he
> should leave his dinner to be
> eaten by a steam engine. He
> cannot be bothered to digest
> his own soul.

The Schlegel sisters, are of course, different from the Wilcox. They do know how to explore their own nature. It is Helen, who talks about the Wilcox's failures most succinctly:

> Perhaps, the little thing that says
> 'I' is missing out of the
> middle of their heads, and
> then it's a waste of time to
> blame them...There are two
> kinds of people-our kind-who
> live straight from the middle
> of their heads, and the other
> kind who can't, because their
> heads have no middle...

It is precisely this sense of "I" that Maurice develops through his acceptance of when homosexuality. He realises his love for Clive after, he gains essential self-knowledge. He rejects Clive's proposal, and feels sense of pain which leads him to internal integrity a new :

> Thus it was that his agony began as
> a slight regret...It worked inwards,
> till it touched the root whence body
> and soul both spring, the 'I' that
> he had been trained to obscure, and
> realised at least, doubled its power and
> grew super human.

"After this crisis", writes Forster, "Maurice became a man." His countenance is even expressive of true stength, rather than an artificial manliness : everyone around him has "a sense of some change in his mouth and eyes and nose." Thus, the "beast" and the "monk" from within finally evolves into a new wholeness :

> Now he had the highest gift to offer.
> The idealism and the brutality that
> ran through boyhood had joined
> at last, and twined into love
> ...it was 'he', neither body or
> soul, nor body and soul, but
> 'he' working through both.

Sometime later, Maurice tells Clive of his new internal connectedness :

> A lot of things hadn't
> joined up in me that since
> have.

His friends, in turn, reveals the growth of his own heart :

> 'I should have gone through
> life half awake if you'd had
> the decency to leave me alone.
> Awake intellectualy, yes,
> and emotionally in a way;
> but here'–He pointed with
> his pipe stem to his heart...

Maurice is unable to understand homosexual–self until his relation with Clive materialises. On the other hand, Margaret of *Howard's End* has made many "connections" before her story; unlike Maurice with his "Slow nature", She can draw sound conclusion from meagre data. She is confident about her sexuality and the main features of her temperament :

> She does not understand herself
> She has some rudimentary control
> over her own growth.

This self-control is very relevant in Forster's philosophy. If pracedes the ability to understand others. Forster puts such creed of his philosophy in the mind of Clive Durham who had discovered it through studying Plato :

'To make the most of what I have'.
Not to crush it down, not vainly
to wish that it was something
else, but to cultivate it in such
way as it will not vex either
God or Man.

Foester wrote a note about *Maurice*, stating that Margaret and Maurice are working at this same task. They must "connect up and use the fragments they are born with." Mourice, of course, is struggling with Fragments that are much "more scanty and bizarre than Margaret's" as Forster points out; none the less, one feels it as essentially his obtuseness that holds him back, whereas her sensitivity sends her hurtling forward.

Howard's End begins with an account of Helen's brief engagement to Paul Wilcox, " a young man out of the unknown." Like Lilia in *Where Angels fear to Tread,* Helen takes up the first opportunity for love that presents itself. In her eagerness for passion and romance, she encounters Paul "halfway, or more than half way." Margarect echoes Forster's qualified approval of physical love when she says to Helen :

'I understand...at least, I understand
as much as ever is understood of
these things.

Margaret knows about the potency and superficiality of flirtations like Paul's and Helen's; she has been the victim of sudden passion for herself :

And she had often 'loved' too,
but only so far as the facts
of sex demanded; mere yearnings
for the masculine, to be dismissed
with a smile

When she comes to know about her husband's shabby treatment of Jacky Bast, she reminds us of yet another crucial link in the chain of connections. In addition to selfknowledge, one needs to think about others, be aware of the existence of others. Clearly, sex and should is not enough; one must express love :

For more mysterious than the
call of sex to sex is the tenderness
that we throw into that call; Far
wider is the gulf between us and
the farmyard than between the
farmyard and the garbage that
nourishes it.

Schelgel sisters are as vulnerable to "the call of sex to" as Henry is. They too have experienced loneliness like most of the single woman. Forster tells us that a woman's sexual appetite are as great as man's ; when Margaret's utterance ends with intently.

Margaret looked intently at the
butler. He, as a handsome young
man, was faintly attractive to
her as a woman-an attraction
so faint as scarcely to be
perceptible, yet the skies would
have fallen if she had mentioned
it to Henry.

Henry's seduction of Jacky in *Howards End* is similar to the sexual act of Maurice's Father. It has been mentioned several times in the posthumous novel. Forster's judgement about the sexuality of Mr. Hall senior is easily understandable, Unlike his interpretation of Maurice's love affairs :

> **Mr. Hall senior had neither**
> **fought nor thought ; there had never**
> **been any occasion; he had supported**
> **society and moved without a crisis**
> **from illicit to licit love.**

Mr. Hall's presenting Henry's love affair as meaningless, made no demands upon him. It does not ask him develop, or provide tenderness for another human being.

Henry and Mr.Hall fail to make important connections. Their attempts at intimacy and warmth remain trivial, when they are mere "transient grossness", rather than the beginnings of genuine personal commitments to others.

In both *Howards End* and *Maurice*, Forster tries to develop a viable approach to human sexualitiy. He shows the intensity of his interest in the morality of sex through a note, particularly when homosexuals were involved. He queries :

> Is it ever right that such
> relationship should include the
> physical? Yes-sometimes. If
> both people want it and both
> are old enough to know what
> they want-yes. I used not to
> think this, but now I do.
> Maurice and Clive would have
> been wrong. Maurice and Dicky

more so.

Mauric and Alec are all right,

some people might never be right.

Paradoxically, his views in the former novel are much more definitive than in the posthumous work, where it is a primary concern. *In the Longest Journey*, Rickie talks about his own writings with his aunt:

'What is the long story about, then ?'

'About a man and a woman who meet

and are happy'.

'Somewhat of a tour de force, I

conclude.'

He frowned. 'In Literature we needn't

intrude our own limitations.'

Lionel Trilling rightly considers *Howards End* as "Forster's masterpiece"–This is the work that actually talks about possibilities of art. Forster that a homosexual author can deal successfully with heterosexual relationship. By contrast, his treatment of the theme of homosexual love in *Maurice* is at times both tortured and ambiguous.

Lytton Strachey writes in a letter to Forster, dated March 12, 1915, :

I do not understand why the

copulation question should

be given so much importance.

It's difficult to distinguish

clearly your views from Maurice's

sometimes, but so far as I

can see, you go much too

far in your disapproval of
it.

This criticism is particularly suited to the presentation of relation between Maurice and Clive. Forster cannot distance himself from his protagonist. Clive remains a sympathetic character as long as Maurice loves him. He is a Cambridge intellectual, who practices "high-minded homosexuality"; based on Platonic ideals, his affair with Maurice involves very little sex :

It had been understood between them
that their love though including the
body, should not gratify it, and the
understanding had proceeded-no
words were used from Clive.

Maurice's first step to evaluate their relation occurs shortly after the idyllic day the two boys spend together:

One afternoon he had a collapse
He remembered that Clive and
he had only been together one
day : And they had spent it
careening about like
fools–instead of in one
another's arms:

Forster's subsequent comment is situated in terms that echo his remarks about the kiss of Helen and Paul in *Howards End;* here. However, he is much more cynical about sex :

Maurice did not know that they
had thus spent it perfectly–
he was too young to detect the

triviality of contact for contact's
sake...

This passage reflects Forster's note about sex between Maurice and Clive being wrong. It also reflects some positive judgement of the relation as a whole :

Later on, when Maurice's love
took second strength, he realised
how well fate had served him.
The one embrace in the darkness,
the one long day in the light and
the wind were twin columns,
each useless without the other.

Clive seems to be eminently suitable lover for Maurice :

He educated Maurice, or rather
his spirit educated Maurice's spirit ;
for they themselves became equal
...Love had caught him out
or btriviality and Maurice out of
bewilderment in order that two
imperfect souls might touch perfection.

Clive wishes that together. Maurice and he will make the crucial connection between the "beast" and the"monk". Forster does not give any indication about the case but continues to write in the hyperbolic fashion :

When the final darkness
descended they would at
all events have lived more
fully than either saint or
sensualist, and would have

extracted to their utmost
the nobility and sweetness
of the world.

Forster does not condemn Clive till the years–the boys spend together draw to a close. Clive reveals his lack of vitality ultimately.

'To forget every thing-even happiness
Happiness : A casual tickling of
someone or something against one self
–that's all. Would that we had
never been lovers: For then, Maurice,
You and I should have lain still
and been quiet."

Maurice's frustration with this "love such as only finer naturs can understand" finally begins to emerge :

They lay side by side without touching.
Presently Clive said, 'It is no
better here. I shall go.' Maurice
was not sorry, for he could not
get to sleep either, though
for a different reason, and
he was afraid Clive might
hear the drumming of his
heart, and guess what it
was.

In Greece, Clive thinks about his approahing heterosexuality on a prophetically bare stage :

He saw only dying light and a
dead land. He uttered no prayer,
believed in no deity and knew

that the past was devoid of
meaning like the present, and
a refuge for cowards.

This symbolic imagery of death and sterility foreshadows Clive's marriage, and Forster's complete withdrawal of sympathy from Clive at the novel's conclusion.

Maurice turns to Dickie Barry for relief from his loneliness and sexual frustration : when Clive dumps him, Forster's attitude towards given homosexual relaitonship appears to be ambivalent again. Initially, he depicts Dickie's care free sensuality approvingly :

The boy, who had been to a
dance before, remained asleep
He lay with his limbs uncovered
He lay unashamed, embraced
and penetrated by the sun.

The relationship seems promising, as Dickie appeals to Maurice's aesthetic sensibilities as well as his passios, . Forster writes :

The lips were parted, the down
on the upper was touched
with gold, the hair broken
into countless glories, the
body was a delicate amber.
To anyone he would have
seemed beautiful, and to
Maurice who reached him by
two paths he became the
world's desire.

Eventually, however, he withdraws his sympathy for

Maurice's response to Dickie with hyperbolic vehemence that parallels his sudden distaste for the platonic relationsip with Clive. Maurice's sexual desires degrade him suddenly.

> His feelings for Dickie required
> a very primitive name. He would
> have sentimentalised once and
> called it adoration, but the
> habit of honesty had grown
> very strong...'Lust'. He said
> the word out loud...

One believes that Forster's own uncertainties about the morality of homosexuality prevented him from writing consistent novel.

Maurice's love for Alec is presented with much greater consistency. This affair starts with lust as well. This time, however, the reltionship fulfills the promise made in *Howards End*, insofar as a "trivial collision" in the dark becomes a means of "opening the doors of heaven." As soon as Maurice lays eyes on Alec, his sexual appetitie finds aroused. He sees Scudder cavorting with two maids, on his way to Clive's house. Later, Maurice is subtly conscious of Alec's presence near the piano, and at the back of a brougham carrying him to London. As Maurice's sexuality arouses, he longs to be outdoor. Like Stephen Wonham of *The Longest Journey,* he feels the beauty and sensuality of the open air :

> Scents were everywhere that
> night despite the cold, and
> Maurice returned via the
> shrubbery, that he might
> inhale the evening primroses.

At the time of his fulfillment, Maurice went through pan-Like rites, and dismised the drawing room asexuality of Clive Durhamn. He re-enters the Penge Home, and Durham notices that he has been crowned, as it were, with primrose pollen. "Borenius, is he not quite bacchanalian ?". She comments Maurice revokes the promises of abstinence he made at Cambridge, reinforced by reminders of the simple pleasures of nature, and gets ready for Scudder. He thinks :

He alone-Clive admonishing,
combined advaneed thought with
the conduct of Sunday scholar.
He wasn't Methuselah
he'd a right to a fling. oh those
jolly scents, those bushes where
you could hide, that sky as
black as the bushes.'

In *Howard's End;* Helen tells Margaret :

'You and I have built up
something real, because it
is purely spiritual. There's
no veil of mystery over us
Unreality and mystery begin
as soon as one touches the
body.'

Helen's attraction to Paul Wilcox and her seduction of Leonard Bast involve "Loneliness and the night, and Panic afterwards." rather than a rational decision on her part Clearly, Helen's emotions have hypnotized her, cast her under a spell from which she cannot escape. Only someone like Wilcox, who possesses "the instinctive wisdom the past alone can bestow" could unravel the mystery of Helen's primitive urges and emotional responses.

In both *Howards End* and *Maurice,* the growth of sexual aspects of one's consciousness represents difficualt stage in the process of "connecting." Forster's ambivalent opinion about sex as an indication of his understanding of complexities. The mysterious aspects of man's sexual appetites are brilliantly dealt with E.M. Forster's novels.

Works Cited

Introduction

Furbank, P.N. ed. E.M.-forster's *Maurice*. Harmondsworth : Penguin Books, 1972.

Toynbee, Philip, "Forster's love story," Gardner, *The Critical Heritage*, p.462.

Chapter–1

Borrello, Alfred E.M. Forster: *An Annotated Bibliography of Secondary Materials.* New Jersey : Scarecrow Press, 1974.

Bowen, Elizabeth. "An Autobiography of a Reader of Forster," *Aspects of E.M. Forster* London : Edward Arnold, 1969.

Bradbury, Malcolm. "Forster", in A.E. Dyson, ed., *The English Novel : Select Binliographical Guides*. London : Oxford Universityi Press, 1974.

Forster, E.M. "George Crabbe and Peter Grimes" in his *Two Cheers for Democracy*. Toronto : Penguin Books, 1974.

– • "Three Anti-Nazi Broadcasts" in his *Two Cheers*, p.42.

– • "Notes on the English Character", in his *Abinger Harvest*, 1936; rpt. Harmondsworth : Penguin Books, 1974.

– • "Society and the Homosexual : The Abonimable crime", The *New Statesman and the Nation.* Oct 31/53, p. 508

Macaulay, Rose. *The Writings of E.M. Forster* London : Hogarth 1938. pp 173-4.

Steiner, George, "Under the Greenwood Tree", *New Yorker*, Oct 9, 1971. rpt in Gardner, *Critical Heritage*, p. 418.

Stone, Wilfred. *The Cave and the Mountain : A study of E.M. Forster.* California : Stanford University Press, 1966-p.124.

Trilling, Lionel *E.M. Forster.* New York : New Directions, 1964.11.

Chapter-2

Forster, E.M. *Maurice,* ed. P.N. Furbank. Harmondsworth : Penguin Books, 1972.

– • "Notes on the English character" in his *Abinger Harvest,* 1936. rpt. Harmondsworth : Penguin Books, 1974.

– • *Goldsworthy Lowes Dickinson.* London : Edward Arnold, 1934.

– • *Where Angels Fear to Tread.* 1905; Toronto : Random House, 1920.

– • *Marianne Thornton : A Domestic Biography.* New York: Harcourt, Brace, 1956.

– • *A Room with a view,* 1908; Toronto : Penguin Books, 1974.

– • *The Longest Journey,* 1907; rpt. Toronto: Random House, 1962.

– • Aspects of the Novel, 1927; rpt. Harmondsworth; Penguin Books, 1972.

Chapter-3

Crews, Fredrick C. *E.M.-Forster : The Perils of Humanism.* London : Oxford University, 1962.

Forster, E.M. *Maurice,* ed. P.N. Furbank. Harmondsworth : Penguin Books, 1972.

– • *Where Angels fear to Tread.* 1905; Toronto : Random House, 1920.

– • *A Room With a view,* 1908; Toronto: Penguin Books, 1974.

– • *The Longest Journey,* 1907; rpt. Toronto : Random House, 1962.

– • *The life to come, and other stories,* ed. Oliver Stallybrass. The Abinger Edition of E.M. Forster , VIII. London : Edward Arnold, 1972.

– • *Goldsworthy Lowes Dickinson.* London : Edward Arnold, 1934.

Stone, Wilfred. *The Cave and the Mountain. : A Study of E.M. Forster.* California : Stanford University Press, 1966.

Chapter-4

Finkestein, Bonnie B. *Forster's Women : Eternal Differences.* New York : Columbia University, 1974.

Forster, E.M. *Maurice,* ed. P.N. Furbank. Harmondsworth : Penguin Books, 1972.

– • *Howards End.* Harmondsworth : Penguin Books, 1974.

– • *Where Angels Fear to Tread.* Toronto : Random House, 1920.

– • *The Longest Journey.* Toronto : Random House, 1962.

– • *A Room with a view.* Toronto : Penguin Books, 1974.

Strachey, Lytton, Letter to Forster, March 12,1915, rpt. in Philip Gardner, ed. E.M. Forster : *The Critical Heritage.* London : Routledge and Kegan Paul, 1973.

Trilling, Lionel. *E.M. Forster.* New York : New Directions, 1964.